The Winds of God
Bring Revival

The Winds of God Bring Revival

by
Norvel Hayes

HARRISON HOUSE
Tulsa, Oklahoma

The Winds of God Bring Revival
ISBN 0-89274-375-1
Copyright © 1985 by Norvel Hayes
P. O. Box 1379
Cleveland, Tennessee 37311

Published by Harrison House, Inc.
P. O. Box 35035
Tulsa, Oklahoma 74153

Contents

PART I
Publisher's Introduction

Wilt thou not revive us again: that thy people may rejoice in thee?

Psalm 85:6

1
Publisher's Introduction

. . . O Lord, revive thy work in the midst of the years, in the midst of the years make known; in wrath remember mercy.

Habakkuk 3:2

What is revival? According to Charles Finney, one of the greatest revivalists of all times, a revival presupposes that the Church is in a backslidden state, and a revival consists in the return of the Church from her backslidings, and in the conversion of sinners.

In a true revival, the very foundations of sin are shaken and broken up. The Spirit of God says:

Then [at Mount Sinai] His voice shook the earth; but now He has given a promise, Yet once more I will shake and make tremble not only earth but also the (starry) heavens. . . . Yet once more, indicates the final removal and transformation of all [that can be] shaken, that is, of that which has been created, in order that what cannot be shaken may remain and continue . . . . For our God [is indeed] a consuming fire.

Hebrews 12:26,27,29 AMP

In a revival, Christians and sinners alike are brought under the deep shaking and convicting power of the Holy Spirit. This spirit of repentance that arises within the heart causes people to cry and weep before God with a brokenness that realizes their utter worthlessness without the Lord. Repentance is the forerunner of true revival: it breaks up the fallow ground.

A revival brings a renewal of obedience to our heavenly Father. It lifts the veil of sin and breaks the power of worldliness in the life of a Christian. It is a wind from heaven that brings the freshness and sweet fragrance of the Holy Spirit with His gifts for the Church. It is the power and influence of the Holy Spirit that enables the believer to live a holy life before God. A revival cleanses the Church from the taint of worldliness.

Revival restores faith. A heart that has been cleansed of sin burns with a renewed commitment to love God and labor for the Kingdom. Altars take on a new meaning as a revived heart seeks a place to weep and moan over lost and dying souls. The Holy Spirit ushers in the spirit of prayer, and intercession breaks forth for the salvation of mankind. (Rom. 8:26.) Arms of faith reach out with compassion, encircling and enfolding people with the healing power of Jesus.

Throughout history, God has used revivals to reconcile man back to Him. One of the greatest revivals of all times was the Azusa Street outpouring that occurred in 1906. In the Azusa Street revival the emphasis was on speaking in tongues and the gifts of the Spirit. This great Pentecostal revival began in a humble mission on Azusa Street in Los Angeles, California.

On the heels of the Azusa Street revival, a great wave of healing began in the 1920s. Alexander Dowie, the father of the healing revivalists, built Zion, a 6,000 acre retreat for the righteous. Out of Zion came some of the most prominent revivalists of the age: F. F. Bosworth, John G. Lake, and Raymond Richie. Other prominent revivalists were evangelists like Smith Wigglesworth and Aimee Simple McPherson.

The 1930s depression hampered the touring ministries of the Zionists. By 1947 the pioneers of the healing revival were all gone, but there was renewed hunger for the divine healings and manifestations of the gifts of the Spirit. So God raised up a new breed. The new revival that sprang up dwarfed the successes of the 1920 revivalists. The Holy Spirit moved on all flesh and drew huge crowds.

The years 1947 to 1952 were ecstatic ones filled with long hopeful nights under big tents with sawdust floors. The air was punctuated with shouts of "praise the Lord" and "hallelujah." Revivalists such as William Branham, Gordon Lindsay, Jack Coe, T. L. Osborn, Oral Roberts, and A. A. Allen were recognized as giants of this era. *The Voice of Healing* magazine, published by Gordon Lindsay, became the mouthpiece of these men.

The level of expectancy was high in this wave of revival. "During these old-time tent meetings, faith filled the hearts of men to believe that the glory would sweep in and fill those big tops and maybe, just maybe, all things truly are possible, only believe."*

In the early sixties, healing revivalism became a lonely business as the big tent revival era began to wane. Yet evangelist David Nunn wrote, "The Holy Spirit has shown me the greatest part is yet to come."

Revival moved to the Holiday Inns and Hilton ballrooms as the Full Gospel Business Men's Fellowship became the new tool God used to stir revival. Soon, a charismatic awakening (of the gifts of the Spirit and tongues) was surging among all denominations.

---

* David Edwin Harrell, J., *All Things Are Possible*, (Ontario, Canada: Fitz Henry, Whiteside, Limited, 1975).

Pentecost jumped the fence as Baptists, Methodists, and Catholics were speaking in tongues and welcoming the gifts of the Spirit. The charismatic revival pushed aside denominational barriers and swept in the message of the full gospel which says: Jesus Christ is the Healer, Savior, and Baptizer in the Holy Spirit. The charismatic revival is still active today.

The purpose of this book is to make you aware of the new wave of revival that is now sweeping the land. We pray that as this story unfolds, you will be encouraged to ride this wave of glory and let it sweep you into a place of hunger for God. Our sincere desire is to place a deep longing for God down in your spirit.

Whatever your state, whether sinner or saint, revival brings a foretaste of heaven to earth. You'll find after being in union with God and abiding in Him, after enjoying the sweetness and peace of His presence, that the charm of this world is completely broken. Once you've tasted the glory, you'll never be satisfied with anything else!

PART II

The Vision —
Revival Like a Mighty Wind
Rushing from Heaven

Then said he unto me, Prophesy unto the wind, prophesy, son of man, and say to the wind, Thus saith the Lord God; Come from the four winds, O breath, and breathe upon these slain, that they may live.

Ezekiel 37:9

2

The Vision: Revival

In 1971 the Spirit of the Lord told me to go to Washington, D.C., to Howard University. This was during the time when they had rioting on university campuses. The students at this university had gathered all the chairs out of the dormitories and carried them downstairs to the front gate where they stacked them so nobody could get onto the campus.

The Lord told me to go there. I'd been working with students on college campuses for years, so I caught a plane from Chattanooga, Tennessee, to Washington, D.C. From the airport, I took a cab to the administration building at Howard University. Carrying my luggage, I went in and talked to the receptionist. I said, "My name is Norvel Hayes. I'm from Tennessee. Do you have a chaplain? God told me to come here."

She said, "Yes. Let me get Reverend Short for you." She returned with the chaplain at her side.

I said, "My name is Norvel Hayes. God told me to come here."

He looked at me and said, "I believe it." He asked, "Where are you staying?"

I answered, "I just got out of a cab from the airport. I'll get a motel here somewhere."

But he responded, "No, we'll get you a place to stay. I believe the Lord sent you here."

He asked if I would like to stay in a home with five Catholic priests.

I said, "Why not?" I figured it would be a good experience.

When Reverend Short took me to the home, he told me, "You're welcome to stay as long as you want. The reason they have an empty bed is that one of their priests just died in it."

I said, "I'm not going to die in it, praise God forever! I came here on a mission. What the mission is, I don't know."

Pat Boone was supposed to speak for chapel service in two or three days. But something happened and Pat couldn't come. The university staff called me and asked me if I'd speak in his place. I said, "Sure, if you want me to."

They told me what time the service was. I went over to the chapel hall which was totally packed. There were hundreds and hundreds of students. I sat on the stage of the auditorium with two black ministers. They invited a young man to sing a solo before they introduced me. As he was singing the solo, the Spirit of God came upon me, and I began to weep.

While I wept, I received a vision from God. In the vision, I saw four winds coming down out of heaven from way up in the heavenlies somewhere. I didn't even know that God had four winds. One came from the east, one from the west, one from the north, and one from the south. All four winds came from different directions out of the heavens.

As they came toward each other, I watched. It was like four whirlwinds, and God let me see it. The four winds came together up in the heavenlies with a force and hit head-on. As they became one great whirlwind, they fell to earth. And the word of the Lord came unto me saying, "This is the way the revival will come to the earth — like the wind, all of a sudden, out of heaven. Nobody will see it — it will just come. And I am going to use young people as a big part to spark the revival. I will use young people to start it."

After He said this to me, I sat there still weeping. As the soloist continued to sing, the word of the Lord came unto me again saying, "When he gets through singing, stand, go to the microphone and prophesy what you've just seen and what you heard. Son, prophesy what you've seen and what you heard."

When the singer finished the song, I got out of my seat, half stumbling and half weeping, and took the microphone. The audience, very attentive, listened closely. I opened up my mouth and began to prophesy what I saw coming down from heaven. I prophesied about the four winds bringing revival to the earth and how God would use young people. I prophesied exactly what I saw and what the Lord had said to me. As I prophesied, it felt like I took a bath inside. I spoke the prophecy out in the Howard University chapel service and the people broke out rejoicing; they were jubilant. Many of them stood weeping and rejoicing.

The next morning I was eating breakfast in the Howard University campus cafeteria. Reverend Short saw me and came over to sit at my table. I'll never forget it as long as I live.

He said, "Mr. Hayes, the Lord has sent you here. The Lord has sent you to this university."

I said, "Yes, I know He did."

He said, "The University executives had a special meeting this morning, they were so moved by the prophecy that you gave yesterday. They have decided to give a couple of Christian boys on campus some money to have meetings on campus, to try and stop the rioting and get the students quieted down. They know that God sent you here to give that prophecy out. They believe with this kind of atmosphere, and because of the way the students responded to you when you spoke to them, that God is the answer to bringing peace to this university. We want you to have some more meetings about God."

Then he said, "God absolutely sent you here to give that prophecy out."

I said, "Oh, I believe that. I believe it now. When I came here, I didn't know what I came for, but God knew."

That was in 1971. I told that prophecy in my teaching for 14 years. Sometimes I told that story and sometimes I told the people, "You might as well look out — there's a revival coming! You might as well look out, because I've already seen it. It's coming, and God is going to use young people to start it and get it sparked."

Then in March, 1985, I went to the Word of Faith Church in Dallas, Texas, to hold a satellite seminar which was supposed to last only four nights. But God had other plans.

First a boy, about 14 years old, received a vision from the Lord. A light came down from heaven and engulfed the Word of Faith Church. The boy saw angels. And he saw what God was going to do.

The next night Valarie Owen, a teacher from Word of Faith Bible School, stood and told of being caught up in the Spirit that morning:

"There was a powerful anointing, while we were praising God. I got on my knees, then went into a trance. I could not move. God said these words to my heart, 'Azusa Street, Azusa Street. You were interceding and breaking powers and I'm going to pour out My Spirit as I poured out my Spirit on Azusa Street. But you haven't seen anything yet.'

"Azusa Street was a church in California where God began to pour out His Spirit, just like at Pentecost. God showed me this group of people were dedicated and determined to get more and more of God. They were hungry. So they got together and they demanded from the Lord. They pulled down power from on high because they believed God. And they stayed, until the power came. They say it came like a mighty rushing wind, just like on the day of Pentecost. When it fell, the people that didn't want it ran. By the time we finish, it will be Azusa Street all over again. Glory to God! Hallelujah!"

The next day little third and fourth graders asked their teachers if they could pray instead of going to recess. They wanted to come down in front of the church and pray. So they came down and started praying, and the whole bunch of them fell out in the Spirit. They just fell out on the floor while they were praying, and kept on praying. They were there for two or three hours. Little kids.

The Lord had told me 14 years before that He would use little kids to spark off the revival. I was sitting on the platform when these testimonies came forth. The Holy Spirit allowed me to relive the prophecy and the vision I'd seen in Washington, D.C., in 1971. He said, "It's coming to pass. This is it. What I told you would happen is happening right before your eyes."

That night I told the people about that vision. All kinds of things started happening, both in the service and outside. People saw signs and wonders from God. They saw visions and fell out and prayed. The phone lines were jammed with testimonies of what God was doing across the country. It was the beginning of the revival that would sweep the earth.

PART III
The Gifts of the Spirit —
God's Weapons for the Church

Now concerning spiritual gifts, brethren, I would not
have you ignorant.

1 Corinthians 12:1

3
God's Gifts Solve Problems

When thousands of people are watching a seminar on TV, you like to teach something that will help them forever. I taught about the gifts of the Spirit at the Dallas seminar because learning about that will help you forever.

I believe your whole life will change if you'll listen to what the Spirit of the Lord says concerning the gifts of the Spirit. The gifts of the Holy Spirit are the answers to all of the world's problems. The gifts of the Spirit are the answers to all of *your* problems.

Always remember this: You will never have a problem in your life that the gifts of the Spirit can't correct and give you information about. They cover all of the problems that you have now or ever will have. If President Reagan had all of the nine gifts of the Spirit operating in his life, his worries would be over because he would know what to do in advance.

Everything you need is in 1 Corinthians 12 — all those beautiful gifts, given out as the Spirit wills. And the Holy Spirit always wills to give them out continually wherever they're taught and wherever they're believed.

The Ministry of the Holy Spirit

The only reason we don't get any more help from God than we do is because we don't know the ministry of the Holy Spirit.

21

The Holy Spirit would make you rich if you'd let Him. But of course, until you learn to handle money, He won't do that. He would heal you if you'd let Him. He knows exactly how to heal you. He'd give you a miracle. The Holy Spirit would create things for you if you'd show God you trust Him to that degree.

If you go to church, you trust God generally. You have a general type faith that believes God can do anything. But as long as you live, remember this: God won't accept that. God won't accept general faith. You have to be specific with God if you want the Holy Spirit to manifest Himself. As long as you walk around saying, "Well, I believe that Jesus could do anything. I believe God could do anything," the Holy Spirit, Who lives in your belly, will just lay there. He'll never manifest Himself even though He has been sent from heaven to bring heaven's blessings to you.

Third John 2 says, . . . **I wish above all things that thou mayest prosper and be in health, even as thy soul prospereth.** In heaven you will see the height of wealth. In heaven they don't even know the meaning of poverty. If you'll work for God in your life, when you get to heaven, you'll probably have diamond doorknobs. There is no poverty in heaven, just like there are no diseases.

You hear people quote, "There are no diseases in heaven, there will be no cripples in heaven, there will be no blind people in heaven." That's right. But also, there will be no poverty in heaven.

The Holy Spirit — the Person Who lives in your belly, thinks exactly like heaven is. He doesn't think any other way. That's where He came from. That's all He's ever known. He is consumed with positive energy creating wealth, health, and miracles. He brings good things to you. He will do anything for you, that is, anything heaven has to offer.

Jesus did a lot of good things, and when He told people He was going away, they got all shook up. But Jesus plainly explained things to them. He said, "No. Don't get shook up because it's good for you that I go away. If I go not away, the Comforter will not come. But when He comes, He will be in you, and He will guide you, and lead you into all truth and teach you." (John 16.)

The Holy Spirit is the Great Teacher. He'll teach you all truth about anything. He's the Teacher of the Church.

In every area of your life where you're not successful, you're not being led by the Spirit of God, because He thinks no other way except success. He's consumed with it. He thinks only about success.

The reason the Church per se is so crippled is because the nine gifts of the Holy Ghost are not in operation as they should be. *The nine gifts of the Spirit are the answer to all the world's problems, every one of them.* Every church in the world is supposed to have all nine gifts in operation allowing the Holy Spirit to give His ministry out as He wills.

The Holy Spirit has a ministry. And He has gifts He wants to give you. The nine gifts of the Holy Spirit are His ministry. They are not your ministry. You can't make *one* gift of the Spirit operate. The gifts of the Holy Spirit are given to a believer as the Spirit wills. (1 Cor. 12:11.) You're the vessel it comes through.

Learn to Receive From Heaven

For you to receive from heaven is the most simple thing in the world, but you have to learn how to do it. You'll never learn with your mind. You have to pray that you'll have the mind of Christ so you can understand the Bible and accept it just the way it's written. God will do great and mighty things for you! He'll do anything for you. It is not God's will that He withhold any good thing from you. It's God's good pleasure to give you your heart's desire and so many gifts that you don't have enough room to contain them. (Ps. 37:4; 84:11; Mal. 3:10.)

You say, "Well, I wish I had some of them."

You can get them. I urge you to seek all nine of the gifts of the Spirit.

It Can Save Your Life

The graveyard is full of people who don't even know what's in 1 Corinthians 12. If you don't know what's in there, it can cost you your life.

One manifestation of the Holy Ghost through one gift can absolutely save your life — just one manifestation. You need to study, learn, and know what all the nine gifts are, and you need every one of them. Don't think you'll ever just need healing and miracles. You need all nine of them.

A time in your life is coming when you're going to be desperate for every one of the nine gifts of the Spirit. And every one of them you leave out, and pay no respect to, or don't spend time learning about, might be just the link that will be missing.

It will be a blessing from Almighty God, coming from heaven to you, that you can't have. God won't give it to you. Every part of the New Testament that you leave out of your life, that's the part you can't have. You have to learn what's in there.

You have to be steadfast. You have to know, that you know, that you know what's in there. And you have to tell God you know what's in there. If you tell God that and tell Him you believe it, He'll give it to you.

He'll manifest Himself and give it to anybody, anywhere. It doesn't make any difference to Him. God's not selfish.

Don't leave a missing link in your life and limit how the Holy Spirit can use you. Learn all you can, because God works only with knowledge.

Gain Understanding

That's the reason it's so important to begin studying, learning, and keeping your own mind renewed with the Word of God after you get born again by the Spirit of God. The Holy Spirit works only through knowledge. And you're not as smart as the Holy Spirit!

You may think you know a lot about God. But when you start getting in tune with the Holy Spirit, He'll let you know there are a lot of things about God you don't know.

Suppose I went out and canvassed 100 pastors from different denominations, lined them up, and tested them on where the gifts of the Spirit were found in the Bible. We'd probably lose 75 of them right then.

If on my next test, I asked them to list the nine gifts of the Spirit, we'd lose 20 more of them. We've got only five left. If I then gave them ten minutes to write the definition of each of the nine gifts of the Spirit and list how they operate, we might possibly have two or three left.

My point is this: God works for the Body through the knowledge of the pastor. As an individual you *can* contact God and believe for yourself, but usually you only believe what they teach where you go to church. If you're Baptist, you usually believe what the Baptists believe. If you're Methodist, you believe what they believe. If you belong to a Catholic church, then you listen to the priest. And if you go to the Church of Christ, you believe what they say.

Study the Word of God. He says, **I change not** (Mal. 3:6). He stays steadfast all the time. God is love and has always been from the Old Testament to the New. Seven of the gifts of the Spirit listed in the New Testament for the Church today also operated in the Old Testament. The only two gifts of the Spirit that did not operate in the Old Testament are tongues and interpretation of tongues. They came into being after the Day of Pentecost, when tongues first visited the 120 in the upper room. (Acts 2.)

If you've never been baptized in the Holy Spirit with the evidence of speaking in tongues, I suggest that you pray and believe God by faith that you have received. Praying in the Holy Ghost opens up your human spirit to the things of God. It also causes you to be more sensitive to the things of God. When you believe God more, then He manifests Himself to you more. It's God's will that you know these things.

The Holy Spirit Says, "Trust God"

Sometimes the Holy Spirit will rise up in me, and the Holy Spirit Himself, not me, will just weep. He said to me after weeping for a long time:

"Oh, son, I want to heal the sick so much. I wish they could trust Me. I wish they would believe Me. I have been sent to the earth to heal them. I've been sent to the earth to stretch their legs out. I've been sent to the earth to open up their blind eyes. I wish they would believe Me and trust Me. And I wish they would praise Jesus, because He's a healer.

"I'll do the work for them. I've been sent here to do the work. But they must trust Me."

It's called faith in God — trust. Remember that: faith trusts God.

Tell people that Jesus heals and that's it. He heals everyone who will believe in Him. Boldly tell them, and He will heal them. Don't be backward and don't be ashamed of it. Always remember: anything you're ashamed of, God won't give to you. If you are ashamed of Jesus the Healer, then Jesus will be your Savior, but He'll never become your healer. Don't be ashamed of it. The bolder you can believe it, the better God likes it. And the more heaven shouts and rejoices, the more the Holy Spirit will rise up within you and give you exactly what you want from God.

". . . Given to Every Man . . ."

Look at 1 Corinthians 12:7. It will keep you free from yourself. It will keep you free from false doctrines. It will keep you free from allowing your mind to think that Jesus might not want you to have the gifts of the Spirit. It says, **But the manifestation of the Spirit is given to every man to profit withal.**

Say out loud, "Every man means me." Believe it! If you'll say that every day, and know that the Spirit has been given to manifest Himself to you personally, then you'll keep all those lies out of your mind. You'll keep all those deceiving spirits from the devil out of your mind.

Remember: the gifts will help you in your business. They'll help you in your relationships. They'll help you in anything that concerns you. One of the nine gifts of the Spirit can solve any problem you have.

4
Teaching Is Vital

God is not lazy; He's diligent. He's not poor; He's very wealthy. He's not ignorant; He's very intelligent. And He does not deal through ignorance. So if you're going to get God to do anything for you, you're going to have to get smart. God does not bless ignorant people; if He did, they wouldn't be ignorant. He will bless you with anything you can stand.

Wherever I go, I suggest to pastors to hold seminars in their churches at least once a year on the gifts of the Holy Spirit. They can teach it themselves or have a visiting minister. Then, I suggest that during the year, as the Lord leads, they preach on one gift some Sunday, then another until they cover all nine.

The more you teach on it, the more you preach on it, the more you talk about it, the more you recognize it, and the more you expound upon it, the more the gifts will work for you. They will come into manifestation for you. All the nine gifts of the Spirit are given to you through the Holy Spirit, as the Spirit wills. And the Spirit always wills wherever the Word is preached.

The Word and the Holy Spirit Agree

If 1 Corinthians 12 is not preached in a given church, then the Spirit doesn't will to give the gifts of the Spirit there. The Holy Spirit is on earth only to confirm the Word with signs following. The Holy Spirit is a first class performer. He performs the New Testament for anybody who will believe it. He has been sent by God, through a prayer that Jesus prayed, to help people, to teach people, and to perform the New Testament. (John 16.) The Holy Spirit will perform any verse that you will believe and not doubt. He'll give it to you. You have to understand that. The Word and the Holy Spirit agree.

You may say, "Well, why doesn't the Holy Spirit do more for me?"

I can tell you really quick. He doesn't agree with your head. You're too far out for Him. If you will remind God of what you believe, then quote chapter and verse, the Holy Spirit will come alive, because He confirms the Word with signs following. And if you will study 1 Corinthians 12 and believe all of it, He'll perform it for you. The Spirit and the Word agree.

The Gifts of the Spirit

First Corinthians 12:1 says, **Now concerning spiritual gifts, brethren, I would not have you ignorant.** The one thing in the Bible that God has asked the Church not to be ignorant of is what they are the most ignorant of — spiritual gifts.

If you're going to deal with God and the gifts of the Holy Spirit, you're going to have to believe 1 Corinthians 12. You're going to have to show respect for it. You have to think it's precious and desire and hunger for all nine gifts of the Spirit. When you do and you believe, they come easily through the Holy Ghost on the inside of you. So keep your human spirit in good

30

enough shape to pick up what the Holy Spirit is trying to do.

When you get born again by the Spirit of God,
your human spirit takes on a new nature, because
Divinity comes to indwell you. The channel God uses
to communicate with your spirit is the Holy Spirit. You
don't know what you need. You only *think* you *might*
know what you need. You know what you need in
some cases, but there will be times in life when you
won't know how to pray. That's when the Holy Ghost
will lead you and guide you into the truth. (John 16.)

Make up your mind to believe God can help you.
Then He'll help you through the Holy Ghost by speaking to your spirit.

You might ask, "Why am I ignorant of the gifts of
the Spirit?"

You are ignorant because you haven't been taught.
And where are you taught the things of God? In
church, of course. If you don't know about the gifts of
the Spirit, then you can't believe in them. If you don't
believe, you can't enjoy and partake of the gifts. God
says the reason you're not enjoying the gifts of the Spirit
is because of what you've been taught in the past.
You've been led away from Him by dumb idols. (v. 2.)

Everything that's not victory to God is a dumb idol.
You may call it a church service, but God doesn't call
it a church service. He calls it getting together and doing
a bunch of nothing. You're led away because you stray
from the directions of the Word of God.

Do the Gifts Operate for Everyone?

**Wherefore I give you to understand, that no man
speaking by the Spirit of God calleth Jesus accursed:**

31

and that no man can say that Jesus is the Lord, but by the Holy Ghost.

Now there are diversities of gifts, but the same Spirit. And there are differences of administrations, but the same Lord. And there are diversities of operations, but it is the same God which worketh all in all.

1 Corinthians 12:3-6

Some people say, "Brother Norvel, it might not be God's will for me to have that, or the Lord might not want to do that for me."

He wants to do it for you where it's preached, and believed, and expounded upon. He wants to do it. If He never hears your faith in 1 Corinthians 12, He never performs it for you. All the nine gifts are free. He wants to give them to you as gifts. That's why they're called *gifts.*

But the manifestation of the Spirit is given to every man to profit withal (v. 7). That means to profit with all heaven has. Glory to God! The gifts are given to every man. He'll give them to *you.* Keep all the doubt out of you, and don't ever say again, "Maybe God doesn't want me to have a miracle or a healing." Yes, He does. It's been provided for you.

You might say, "Well, the gifts of the Spirit don't work for everybody."

That's not what the Bible says.

Now there are times when God will manifest a gift powerfully through an individual for public ministry. I used to work in large conventions with Kathryn Kuhlman. She gave me a special pass to come to her meetings anytime I wanted. Sister Kuhlman was a woman who found favor with God. He gave her two strong gifts: the word of knowledge and the gifts of healing. These gifts were very strong in her ministry. She also had the gift of working of miracles operating in her services. Her whole ministry was built on these gifts, and she protected them by not allowing anything to come between her and the Holy Spirit.

That's probably why the gifts operated so strongly — she protected them with her life! She called down immediately anybody who tried to interfere with them. In every service the gifts would flow. Hundreds of people were healed and saved. Sinners sat there and watched her services for hours. Lots of times they would get healed in the overflow. I've been to services of hers that lasted five or six hours. The Holy Ghost would start working. It was something else.

But the same word of knowledge that Kathryn Kuhlman had to minister in public, you can have yourself on a lesser scale as you need it. It's available for you. God didn't write the Bible for some people and not for others. God didn't give nine gifts of the Spirit to the Church for just some people. But He does choose some people to minister those things in public under a special anointing.

God has called me and given me a particular gift of working of miracles to operate in my ministry: people receive new hearts from God. You could come forward and not get one if you boldly just wouldn't believe God. But probably 95 percent of the people who come forward to get a new heart, get one. That started operating in my ministry in 1971. I was in the back seat of a car in Carbondale, Illinois, on my way to a meeting and God gave me that gift of healing.

Sometimes my heart will begin to hurt, and it will hurt for an hour or two. It will hurt so bad, I'll have to lay my hand over my heart. And the Lord will say, "You'd better obey me tonight." I'll call people down for new hearts, and He just pumps new hearts into their chests.

The Gifts Operate to Profit Humanity

Verse 7 will deliver you from all doubt and from your religious background if you'll let it. Now read verse 8:

> For to one is given by the Spirit the word of wisdom; to another the word of knowledge by the same Spirit; to another faith by the same Spirit; to another the gifts of healing by the same Spirit;
>
> To another the working of miracles; to another prophecy; to another discerning of spirits; to another divers kinds of tongues; to another the interpretation of tongues: But all these worketh that one and the selfsame Spirit, dividing to every man severally as he will.
>
> **1 Corinthians 12:8-11**

God does things through the Holy Ghost as He wills. It's something that *God* does. You can't make the healing power of God come upon you. But if you just talk about it, it will come, because the Lord says, "I'll go with you and confirm the Word with signs following."

You can't make the healing power of God come upon you, but if God has given it to you (and your ministry *is* a gift), it will always come whenever you teach on it. But sometimes it will be ten times stronger than at other times.

To get your mind straightened out so you can see the whole Body of Christ needs every one of the gifts, read verse 18 closely: **But now hath God set the members every one of them in the body . . . .**

God has sent all of the nine gifts of the Spirit to be given to the Church by the Holy Ghost. The last part of that verse says . . . **as it hath pleased him.** It pleased Him to give the gift of the word of knowledge to Kathryn Kuhlman. It pleased Him to give me the gift of working of miracles to get people new hearts. The gifts operate to profit humanity. God chooses the ministry gift and, by His will, decides what gift will operate.

I don't know why He chooses certain people. It is as *He* wills, not as you or I will. Sometimes God sends me a thousand miles to bring one message in tongues at some convention somewhere.

Why does He do that? I have no earthly idea. There are probably 500 people there who could speak in tongues — I have no earthly idea why He would send me. But sometimes He does. This is one of the gifts God has given me to minister in public.

> But now hath God set the members every one of them in the body, as it hath pleased him. And if they were all one member, where were the body? But now are they many members, yet but one body. And the eye cannot say unto the hand, I have no need of thee: nor again the head to the feet, I have no need of you.
>
> **1 Corinthians 12:18-21**

This means you need all nine gifts in manifestation, not just one. Don't get lopsided — seek all the gifts.

Study to Show Yourself Approved

Study the Word of God and show yourself approved. Show God that you believe the Bible. You can't believe it unless you study it. Any part of the Bible you show God you believe, He will give to you. You don't have to show people anything, but you have to show God.

You have to show God you believe the book of Galatians. You have to show Him you believe the book of Luke. If you don't, you can't have it. God won't give it to you. God says you have to remind Him of the scripture that you're standing on — remind Him of the words you believe. (Is. 43:26.) For the rest of your life, you have to remind Him. Pick out a scripture that covers your case and remind Him.

Get the Gifts Flowing

Pastors must remind God about the nine gifts of the Spirit: Word of wisdom, word of knowledge (and understanding), gift of faith, working of miracles, gifts of healing, prophecy, divers tongues, interpretation of tongues, and discerning of spirits. Tell God you want all of them. Tell God, "I believe in all nine of them." Remind God of the book of Corinthians. If you don't do that, the gifts of the Spirit begin to wane and die and do not manifest themselves. Then you get into a religious rut.

If you are a pastor, take your Bible into the sanctuary in the afternoon when nobody's there, and open it up to 1 Corinthians 12. Lay it on the floor. Get on your knees over it. Stare at it. Make up your mind that you want the nine gifts of the Spirit in your church.

Start praying and claim all nine gifts of the Spirit. Walk the floor like Elisha, to and fro. Hold up the Bible and tell the Lord you want these gifts. Cry out in a loud voice, "Oh, God, I want these nine gifts of the Spirit for my people, for my congregation. They have a right, Jesus. They have accepted You, Jesus, in their life, and they have a right to be blessed from heaven. And I want all nine gifts of the Spirit to operate in this church, Jesus." (If you are not a pastor, take the same principle and get the gifts flowing.)

If you'll tell God you want the gifts, the Holy Ghost will have the freedom and right to manifest them in your church. And the Holy Ghost will start giving out His ministry through the gifts. He may call one person and lay it upon him or her to speak in tongues in public, or He may give someone the supernatural gift of knowledge.

Every Church Gets the Gospel They Preach

When God hears 1 Corinthians 12, He's ready to manifest it. If you are a pastor, I'm telling you again: Teach your people on the gifts. Hold revivals. Teach seminars. If you don't, it won't be long before you begin thinking, *I've been preaching in my church for years, and God never comes down and heals anybody here. I wonder why?*

I can tell you why. Every church in the world always gets from heaven the type of gospel they preach.

If you leave out 1 Corinthians 12 and the gifts of the Spirit, the Holy Spirit won't perform them in that church much. If you leave out preaching salvation, the Holy Spirit won't save anybody much. He'll do all He can, but not much. If you leave out preaching healing, He won't heal very many people. Whatever you preach on, the Holy Spirit is right there to confirm and do for those who believe it. He'll start manifesting Himself through the gifts of the Spirit.

So then faith cometh by hearing, and hearing by the word of God (Rom. 10:17). Faith in any of God's provisions comes by hearing. When I first came into the full gospel movement, God told me to begin a study about faith. He said, "I'll lead you into other things later." And He did. I was faithful. I'd study and study until He unfolded His Word to me. So when I started teaching on the gifts of the Spirit, it wasn't very long until He started manifesting them.

God will do the same for you. Lay hands on the sick. If you don't feel a thing, claim it by faith. Faith praying is so important. If you don't know what faith is, you can't get much done. Some people don't get an instant manifestation. That was true even when Jesus laid hands on people. — (See Luke 17:12-19.) It is our responsibility to teach them how to receive by faith.

Faith is believing something you don't see. (Heb. 11:1.) Faith is not seeing. It is not touching. In John 20:29, Jesus said to Thomas (who we call Doubting Thomas), **Thomas, because thou hast seen me, thou has believed: blessed are they that have not seen, and yet have believed.**

That's what faith is — believing something you don't feel, touch, or see. Only believe and you will see the glory of the Lord.

When you believe it and are listening really close, it will come. All of a sudden, right out of the clear blue sky, the Holy Spirit will fall on somebody and begin to heal them openly.

It could happen anywhere across this great country. Don't be surprised if a cripple sitting beside you just gets up and walks off. Don't be surprised if a blind person stands up and says, "I can see, I can see!" Don't be surprised if a deaf person beside you stands up and yells, "I can hear everything — everything!" . . . **with God, all things are possible** (Matt. 19:26).

When the Spirit of God flows, whatever work He's doing flows and flows. Sometimes I've known God to heal sinners. At times the power will fall and get on everyone. You *get* the Gospel you *preach*.

The Working of Miracles

In one of my services in 1983, the Lord gave a little girl new feet. The doctors said she could never walk, but she walked that night!

Her parents were a Church of Christ couple. They had never been to a service like this before in their lives. They came only because somebody had nerve enough to give them a set of my tapes.

But that father said, "I believe if I could get my daughter in front of Norvel Hayes, God would heal her." He believed it before he ever came. He heard that I was coming to this church, so he brought his daughter, and God gave her new feet. That was a miracle. The little thing just walked all around there.

Another great miracle of God happened in that same meeting. A couple in the congregation had a child who was going to have a kidney transplant the next morning. When they saw God's miracle, they said, "If God would give that little girl new feet, why does our 12-year-old son have to be cut open and have a kidney transplant? God could give him new kidneys."

They went to the hospital, took the child, and brought him into the service, down front. I walked over and laid hands on him. I asked the Lord to perform a miracle for him and give him a new kidney. The couple took their son back to his hospital room.

The next morning, the doctor took another x-ray before the operation. The nurse walked into the room and asked the parents, "What's happened to this child?"

They said, "What do you mean?"

She said, "This child does not need an operation. He has two new kidneys!"

That's the gift of the working of miracles. The Spirit confirmed the Word with signs and wonders.

The Gifts on Campus

Once I was asked to hold a seminar at Southern Illinois University in Carbondale, Illinois. That university with 22,000 students called me and asked if I would come and teach from the Bible twice a day.

I said, "Why do you want me to come and hold a Bible seminar in a state university?"

One of the officials said, "The university is neutral. We believe in giving everybody the same chance. Our plan is to give up our classrooms for a week to allow different people to come in and teach freely on many topics. In one room witchcraft will be taught. In another, there will be a homosexual play. One of our teachers suggested we give a classroom to Jesus. That is why we called you. We heard you were wild enough to come."

We all know I'm wild, so I went. And I'll never forget that time in my life as long as I live. The people in Carbondale, Illinois, will never forget it either.

Some days I taught a Bible lesson; some days I held a healing service. I'd say, "How many of you have ever seen Jesus heal someone? Well, come tomorrow night, and you'll see the Lord heal people right here."

They piled in — they wanted to see that. Most of them had never seen the laying on of hands in their life. And, of course, God healed them everywhere all over the classroom.

One day a psychiatrist at the university walked in and said, "My patients won't leave me alone. They said I should come over and hear you. They said, 'Doctor, we know that you're the university psychiatrist, but there's a fellow teaching in one of the classrooms who we believe knows some things that you don't know.' "

One of his patients had been really bold and told him, "I've been messed up now for about 15 years. I'm coming to you, and I'm still messed up." That shook him up.

The psychiatrist told me, "Mr. Hayes, I have to leave at 11 o'clock because I have a board meeting at the university."

I said, "OK."

He said again, "I will stay one hour."

So at 11 o'clock I was teaching and nobody left. By 11:30 nobody had left. At noon nobody had left. I closed up the service a little past noon.

The psychiatrist walked up and said, "I couldn't leave. Never in my life have I heard anybody talk like you. I must say it's much more interesting than a university board meeting. Also, I must say that I have never sat two hours anyplace without smoking a cigarette. I must talk with you. I want an appointment with you for one hour."

I said, "When do you want it?"

He said, "I'm the one who wants the appointment, so you name the time and I'll be there."

I told him where I was staying and said, "Meet me this afternoon at 4 o'clock. That way, after I finish talking with you, I'll have a couple of hours to pray through before I go back to the service."

He said, "I'll be there."

At 4 o'clock the university psychiatrist walked in and said, "I'm not believing that I'm here."

I replied, "Well, you *are* here. I can help you if you'll let me."

He stammered, "Ah, well, that's what I came for. I want to let you help me."

"All right. Let me tell you, doctor, I know that you're a very intelligent man. And I know you've got all those degrees. But, let me first suggest that you pull all of that intellectual knowledge out and lay it down.

Just act like you don't have any sense. Act like you're a little boy wanting to learn something. I'm not sure I can answer all your questions, but I'll try. If you will, you can get delivered from yourself."

He said, "I beg your pardon?"

The next sentence rolled out of my spirit. "That way you won't have to leave your office like you've been doing for the past 20 years and head for the country club where you sit and drink your cocktails, listen to dirty jokes, then look at the bottom of your cocktail glass and wonder: 'Is this what life is all about?' "

He gasped, "My God! I've been doing that for 20 years!"

"I know it. Sure you have. That's the reason you're messed up. That's the reason you want to ask a lot of questions." That was the word of knowledge operating. By the Spirit, I read his life story. We spent our hour together. I ended the session with the question, "Are you coming to the service tonight?"

He said, "Are you kidding? I wouldn't miss it."

I spoke that night on the baptism of the Holy Spirit and healing. I gave an invitation for healing first. The psychiatrist jumped up out of his seat and ran down front. He was the first one there. He looked at me and said, "I want to be healed."

I said, "Well, all right."

Then I gave an invitation for the baptism of the Holy Spirit. He raised his hand right in the middle of the invitation and said, "Yeah, that's me! I want that, I want more power, Mr. Hayes!"

Everybody started laughing at him. He turned around to see what they were laughing about.

I said, "Doctor, just take it easy. I guarantee as anxious as you are, you're going to get it."

So he got saved, healed, and baptized with the Holy Ghost all in one night, because the gifts of the Holy Spirit were proclaimed.

Wonder-Working Power

I think the greatest gift of the working of miracles and the gifts of healing I've ever seen manifested happened while I was speaking in Florida. In fact, Brother Kenneth Hagin said, "Norvel, that's one of the greatest miracles I've ever seen. It's probably one of the greatest in this century." Here's the story.

In 1976 I was speaking for Ken Sumrall at the Liberty Bible College auditorium in Pensacola, Florida, one Sunday morning. There were probably about 1,000 people there. I was speaking from Matthew 16:18. I read the scripture, **. . . I will build my church; and the gates of hell shall not prevail against it.** Then I started firing away, saying, "God has given His name, His Son's name, and His power to the Church." I kept saying over and over, "God's got power for the Church."

While I was speaking, I noticed a woman sitting at the back of the auditorium in a wheelchair. She was a scrawny, little blind woman, all twisted up. I had never seen her before in my life.

The Lord said, "Lay your hands on her."

I asked the congregation to excuse me and headed toward the back of the church. I reached out to lay my hands on her and started to pray. The moment the ends of my fingers touched her forehead, God's power, like a whirlwind, picked her up out of the wheelchair and shot her through the air. I was standing in front of an empty wheelchair praying for it. She was gone. I was as shocked as anyone there.

By the time I turned my head to find her, she was already normal, walking and running around. Later, she gave her testimony. She said she was a cerebral palsy case: blind, mind deranged, and pathetically crippled. Her family had placed bars around her bed. But now, her mind was sound. Every twisted, crooked limb was perfectly normal. She was running around, praising the Lord. The gifts are for the Church.

Today this woman goes around the country holding healing meetings. She's been on TV. I didn't even know God did things like that. I'd never seen God do anything like that before. For years, I watched Oral Roberts lay hands on people at his tent meetings. I knew God healed them, but I had never heard of God coming in, picking up and shooting through the air in a split second a crippled, twisted, mindless saint. In an instant, He made everything about her normal.

That's what you call the gift of the working of miracles *and* the gifts of healing. It's a double dose. It's a gift to the Church, a gift of the Church. We would see the Holy Spirit manifest more if we would spend time in the sanctuary praying and calling Jesus a miracle worker and a healer. God just loves for you to call Him a healer. And if you'll call Him a miracle worker, He'll become your miracle worker. The Spirit confirms the Word.

5

Obedience Manifests the Gifts

The first time the gift of faith ever operated through me was in Chattanooga, Tennessee, at a Full Gospel Business Men's meeting. The chapter president's wife was sickly and needed to go to Florida to spend every winter. She was a very weak woman, extremely thin and very pale. She could only eat baby food or little, light things. That night, at the end of the service, she came up and got in the healing line. I prayed for her and she sat down. When I got to the end of the line, I turned around and noticed she was sitting there with her head down like she wasn't healed.

The only way I can explain what happened next is that I felt like the Popeye cartoon character. Popeye was just a regular sailor until he ate his spinach. Then he became very strong.

I didn't know anything outstanding was going to happen to me. I had no earthly idea what the Holy Ghost was going to require of me. But I had been telling God for about a year, "God, I'll do anything for you, just show me. I'll just do anything for you."

I turned around and saw that woman sitting there. When my eyes fell on her, I saw her healed. An abundance of power shot through me, and I changed into another human being. I walked over to her and said, "Helen, what are you doing here with your head down, acting like you're not healed? I prayed for you in Jesus' name and laid hands on you. Why aren't you standing up rejoicing and shouting because you're healed in Jesus' name? Helen, why don't you stand up and claim your healing?"

I was screaming at her. Then she rose up out of her seat and yelled, "I'm healed, I'm healed, I'm healed!"

At that moment, all the power left me and I was just Norvel Hayes again. She was standing there on cloud nine screaming, "I'm healed, I'm healed, Jesus, I'm healed! Thank You, Lord!"

Remember this: God can put power in you in abundance and leave it as long as He wants. He controls it — you don't. You're just there, an obedient vessel for the Holy Ghost to work through. *You* can't make the Holy Ghost do anything.

I was just standing there, all power gone. And the devil said to me, "You're crazy. They'll never invite you to come back here and speak again. What are you doing, screaming at women?"

My mind was giving me fits. Finally I said to myself, "What made me do that?"

About a week later, I saw Helen again. She ran up to me and said, "Norvel, I'm totally healed! I've gained about nine pounds. I went out and ate a T-bone steak that night. Norvel, do you remember about a week ago when you were screaming at me?"

I said, "Oh, God, yes. Don't remind me."

She said, "While you were screaming at me, power came from you into me and the disease left me. That power knocked it out of me!"

You say, "Boy, you have a good ministry, Brother Norvel." That wasn't me. That was the gift of faith — a power gift — surging through me. I saw her healed — I had power in my fingers, power all over me.

Interaction of the Gifts

The nine gifts of the Spirit come in three categories: the power gifts, revelation gifts, and vocal gifts. The power gifts are faith, miracles, and healing. The revelation gifts are the word of knowledge, word of wisdom, and discerning of spirits. The vocal gifts are prophecy, tongues, and interpretation of tongues.

The gift of faith is not the ordinary faith you learn from the book of Hebrews. You build your faith on the book of Hebrews and you learn how to believe God from the whole Bible. That's general type faith. If you want God to manifest Himself, be specific. Remind Him of the scripture you're standing on. However, that's not the gift of faith I am talking about.

The gift of faith is an abundance of power that's manifested to you to get the job done.

It causes you to do something that God wants done when you don't have the knowledge or power to do it. In that case, the gift of faith drops into your spirit and you explode with power. Often the gift of knowledge works with it. You'll find out many times, two or more gifts will work at the same time. In a split second, one, two, three, four, or five gifts could all come into operation. For example, the word of wisdom and knowledge could come, then God could give you the gift of faith to perform a miracle.

After it's all over, you didn't know you were so smart. You're just like me, though — you're not too hot. But the Holy Ghost, Who lives inside of you, knows exactly how to do things. All nine gifts of the Spirit are free gifts to you, if you *believe* they are free gifts. And if you believe that, you've got them.

". . . By His Hands"

The gifts are the ministry of the Holy Spirit, but He uses human vessels. He used Jesus as a human vessel. Jesus was a man just like us. He was made with flesh, blood, and bones. He had to yield Himself to the Spirit of God, and let the Spirit of God work through Him. And it stunned the people. It startled them. Look at Mark 6:1:

> And he went out from thence, and came into his own country; and his disciples followed him. And when the sabbath day was come, he began to teach in the synagogue: and many hearing him were astonished, saying, From whence hath this man these things? and what wisdom is this which is given unto him, that even such mighty works are wrought by his hands?

Wisdom is given to you when you need it by the Holy Spirit.

Look closely at our text. They began to wonder, "What causes this wisdom to come to Him? What wisdom is this that even such mighty works are wrought by His hands? Where does He get that kind of wisdom? We don't do such mighty works in this church. We don't do that in this synagogue."

Where did Jesus get His wisdom? Where did the power come from?

It's simple. God gave Him the wisdom and the hands to deliver the power. God chose hands to work mighty works of God, just like the verse said: **. . . even such mighty works are wrought by his hands.** God has chosen hands to be used for His mighty power to flow from one person to another person. And when God gives it to a person, it will flow from that person to you.

In the early 1970s, I was speaking to a Full Gospel Business Men's Fellowship in Pennsylvania. A man got out of his seat, walked down front, and challenged me. He was a Pentecostal leader of that city.

He said, "I didn't even know what was wrong with me until I came here. I've been deaf for over 30 years."

The word of the Lord came unto me saying, "Cast that deaf spirit out of him."

I walked over to him and said, "You foul, deaf spirit, in Jesus' name, come out of him!"

The moment I said that, he fell, face first, on the floor. Hideous, goofy sounds began to come out of him.

After a while, the sounds stopped coming out of that Pentecostal leader. He raised up and began to laugh. He laughed and laughed.

Finally, I said, "What are you laughing about?"

He said, "I can hear my watch tick. I've been looking at it for 30 years, but I never heard it tick before."

He kept on laughing. "I've been looking at it for 30 years, but it sounds so funny. I didn't know it sounded like that — it sounds like it's racing."

I guess if you had never heard a watch tick and finally heard one, it would be funny to you, too. It was funny to him. He kept on laughing. I said, "Go ahead and laugh, praise God forever. Your ears are open."

Demons Like Your Flesh

The devil operates through your mind and your flesh. You can have a deaf demon in you for 30 years and still love the Lord with all your heart. The demon is not in your spirit, it's in your flesh.

The devil just loves to work through your flesh. He likes for you to commit adultery. He likes for you to take dope to make your flesh feel good. He likes for you to drink a bottle of Jack Daniels — a whole bottle — to make you feel good. He likes for you to eat four pieces of coconut pie and get bigger than a house. Anything the devil can do to your flesh to mess you up, that's exactly what he's going to do. And if you don't stop him from working through your flesh, then he will destroy certain parts of you.

He might pick your ears. On another person, he might pick their eyes, or in another person he might decide to attack the liver. But I've got news for you. If you will believe that a gift of the Spirit called the gifts of healing is for you, God's mighty healing power can make one pass and heal you totally: mind, body, and spirit.

When I obeyed God in Pennsylvania that cold, winter night, that deaf demon left that precious Pentecostal and his ears popped open. When those around him saw the miracle, they jumped up out of their seats and ran down front, reaching out to me, asking me to lay my hands on them. When I reached my hands out and touched them, they fell flat on the floor.

They began to fall back into the chairs. I'd walk back through the aisles, and they'd fall between the chairs. There were more in the back who were trying to get to me. That power was on me. I walked around the room, like a running machine gun, and shot the whole banquet.

An old, white-headed Pentecostal missionary was there. He walked up to me and said, "Son, I haven't seen anything like this in 55 years. Back in the early days of Pentecost, I used to see the power like this. But I haven't seen anything like this in 55 years."

I could have told him I'd never seen it before in my *life.* But I've been seeing it ever since then.

You say, "Did you pray for it, Brother Norvel, or did you just fellowship with the Lord?"

No, it just came. I had told God I was willing to do whatever He wanted me to do.

Yield Yourselves to God

Neither yield ye your members as instruments of unrighteousness unto sin: but yield yourselves unto God, as those that are alive from the dead, and your members as instruments of righteousness unto God.
Romans 6:13

That Christmas, in a Holiday Inn ballroom in Pennsylvania, God put His healing power in my hands. It's been there ever since. I tell Him, "Lord, I'll go lay hands on anybody You tell me to. I'll buy my plane ticket and go anywhere in the world. All I want to do, Jesus, is just what You want me to do, as long as You want me to do it. Then I want to come to heaven and be with You for all eternity.

53

"I'm not interested in doing my own thing, I just want to do what You want me to do. And I want to do it in the way that You want me to do it. I don't want to dream up a bunch of ideas, and a bunch of ministries that You're not in. I'm not interested in that, God. I just want to offer You myself. Anything I have is yours. If there's anyway that You want to use me, just feel free. Missions, one-on-one, TV, or anything else — it doesn't make any difference to me. Just go ahead and use me. I'm available."

Look at your hands. The last 11 words Jesus spoke before He went back to heaven, were: **They shall lay hands on the sick, and they shall recover** (Mark 16:18). The Spirit of God flows from one person to another person. He wants to use your hands.

Joy Inside You Means God Is Pleased

God won't shove anything down your throat. He's definitely trying to get revival to the churches. He wants it to start and spread quickly around the world. He started it in Dallas. He wants to use *you* to spread it to *your* city.

Obedience pleases God. Sometimes the Holy Spirit blesses me with so much joy I can't even study the Bible. He bubbles up inside me with joy. Always remember: when the bubbling of joy comes from inside you, it means heaven, Jesus, and the Holy Spirit are pleased. Obedience pleases God. Sometimes He demands it. At other times, He wants you to choose to be obedient because you love Him.

He wants to use you. Are you available?

As you read the following prayer, put out your hands to receive the healing power of God.

Heavenly Father, in Jesus' name, let Your healing power flow right now into the hands of the person reading this. I pray that it flows mightily in the name of the Lord Jesus Christ. And Lord, this person will use the wisdom of God. He'll lay his hands on sick people and Your mighty power will heal them. In Jesus' name. Amen.

6
Healing Follows
All the Gifts of the Spirit

I've had God to give me a word of knowledge and cause a supernatural healing. I've had God to tell me to speak in tongues, and cause a healing to be manifested in another country to save a person's life.

God heals many people through a prophecy. Did you ever stop and think about that? The healing power of God follows faith. It works like a twin brother with the gift of the working of miracles. Jesus is a healing Savior and the Lord of miracles. Healing follows all the gifts of the Spirit.

God does not want you to be ignorant of any of the nine gifts of the Spirit — especially the gifts of healing. Nearly the whole world is sick, God hates sickness. He loves people, but He hates sickness. Sickness comes from the devil. It causes you heartaches, and it costs you all of your money. Many people go broke because of diseases.

First Corinthians 12:1 says: **Now concerning spiritual gifts, brethren, I would not have you ignorant.** Let me replace "spiritual gifts" with one of the gifts: "Now concerning *healing,* brethren, I would not have you ignorant."

God does not want the Church to remain ignorant concerning healing. Jesus is your personal healer. Refuse to be ignorant. Keep your spirit and mind open to the truth. And the truth is this: Jesus loves you and wants to heal you. Jesus never refused to heal anybody that came to Him and asked for it. Have a hunger for healing. He will not refuse you.

Why can't people believe in healing? It's because of the way their minds and their spirits have been trained in the past. If you spent a lot of time with Jesus and watched Him, you would believe that He is your healer. And when you believe that He is your healer, *He is.* If you believe that He is your miracle worker, He is. If you believe that He will lift you out of the wheelchair, He will. He will make your crooked leg straight. Show faith. Then give action to your faith by pressing in towards Him. If you do, you will be healed.

Pressing-In Faith

The first time I went to Jerusalem, I was to speak at a Full Gospel Business Men's convention. They put me in a suite of rooms in the Diplomat Hotel there.

At three o'clock in the morning, the first night I had ever slept in Jerusalem, God woke me. I heard that sweet, little, still voice say to me, "Get up and pray, get up and pray."

I got out of bed and went out into the living room part of the suite. There was a little table in the room, so I knelt by it. I prayed in tongues. The Bible says to pray in the Spirit when you're not sure how to pray. (Rom. 8:26.) I had no earthly idea what I was to pray about. When you pray in the Spirit, you let the Spirit of God pray through you. He knows everything about everything.

After I had prayed for 30 to 45 minutes, the whole room suddenly filled with God's holy presence.

It happened as quickly as you could bat your eyes. I couldn't stand it. I broke and began to weep. I wept until I was delivered from myself.

What does that mean?

That means you get into God's holy presence so powerfully that your mind becomes quiet. Believe me, most humans need to quiet their minds so God can get heaven's blessing to them. It's amazing the power that's involved when you come to Him and press into Him.

As I lay quietly before God, the Word of the Lord came unto me. It was a gift of the Spirit called the word of knowledge. The Lord said, "Son, tomorrow when you get up to speak, I want you to tell these people, Jew and Gentile alike, that I am the Living God and there is no other. Also, son, tell them to beware of false gods."

I said, "OK, Lord, I will."

The next day I got up and spoke. I said that Jesus is the true and Living God, and there is no other. I warned all of them, Jew and Gentile alike, to beware of false gods.

They sat there and listened, receiving from God.

Then the word of the Lord came to me again saying, "Now then, son, tomorrow I want you to teach them about faith and healing."

So the next day, I got up and taught on faith and healing. I said, "If you trust God, show Him you have faith in Him. Let your faith have action. Show God you have faith in Him."

At the end of the service, I taught on healing. I told the people, "If you believe Jesus will heal you, then *show* God you believe Jesus will heal you. If you want to be healed, get up out of your seat and come down in front right now. Jesus wants to heal you."

A guy lurched up out of his seat. He wobbled toward the front on a twisted leg, pressing in towards the rostrum. The moment he reached the platform, he threw up his hands, let out a yell, and fell flat on the floor.

I didn't know anything about him. I had never seen him before in my life. He stayed on the floor about 10 or 15 seconds. When he jumped up, he was restored. He shouted, "Jesus has healed my leg! I'm normal, I'm normal!"

Do you know why I believe Jesus did that for him? He had exactly the kind of faith that the woman with the issue of blood had in Mark chapter 5. She made up her mind that Jesus was her healer and her provider. She pressed in through the crowd to get to Him. That's pressing-in faith — that kind of faith won't take "no" for an answer.

When you pray, you need to break into the presence of God. Again, that's pressing-in faith. The way you do that is to worship and praise your way out of your natural state of mind until you sense His presence strongly. That way, you can hear the voice of God when it comes.

Divine Healing Power

Jesus talked to me once about His healing power. He called it "divine healing power."

"What does that mean?" you might ask.

That means His healing power is very sacred to Him. It's a very precious thing. When it flows into you, it will drive all diseases out. It can make you totally clean, and totally free from disease by just passing through you one time. It can pass through you one time and straighten your crooked leg. It's amazing, the amount of power that's involved.

When you come to Him and press into Him with the right kind of attitude, He releases that power. I can't make God release healing power to you. I can't make Jesus do that.

But I can speak to you, teach you, get your attention, and build your faith to believe it for yourself. If I can get you to come to Jesus with sincerity, God's power will flash through you. And it's all free.

I've had the Holy Ghost weep through me, because He couldn't heal someone.

"What do you mean?" you ask. "God can heal *anyone.*"

You need a certain amount of respect for God's divine healing power. If you don't believe that Jesus is your personal healer and loves you enough to heal you and give you a miracle, you will stay in the state you are in.

You need to get up every morning and scream to the heavens, "Jesus is my healer. The healing power of God is welcome in this house. Jesus is my healer."

If you would do that every day, He would heal you. He would heal anybody. But you have to *do* it. You can't just think about doing it and get lazy and nonchalant. It won't work. God will not accept nonchalant faith. God does not bless lazy or stingy people.

Agree with God

Boldly stand in front of the whole world and say, "I believe Jesus is my healer."

Say it again and again. God loves it. Jesus loves it. Even if you just said it because I told you to, by the time you say it about 200 times, you'll start believing it. The Holy Spirit starts rising up in you. He works with the truth. He agrees totally with Matthew, Mark, Luke, and John. If you'll think like Mark, the Holy Spirit will agree with you.

The Gifts of Healing

The Bible calls it the *gifts* of healing not the gift of healing. It's plural because God gives many different kinds of healing and gets it to you in many different ways. Sometimes God anoints a ministry gift with a certain type of healing gift. For example Brother Kenneth Hagin has great success with getting people healed from tumors. Or healing can be transmitted by the laying on of hands, or by anointing with oil.

The thing to remember is: It is as the Spirit wills. When 1 Corinthians 12 is preached, taught, and expounded upon boldly in the sanctuary, the gifts will often spontaneously manifest. Someone sitting in the sanctuary might be healed. The gifts of the Spirit operate as God wills, and the Spirit *always* wills.

One time the Lord sent me to speak to about 2,500 missionaries. They were having a missionary convention in Roy Stockdale's church in Baton Rouge, Louisiana.

I was speaking one night when, all of a sudden about 15 rows back, five or six people stood and began to talk excitedly.

I said, "What's happened back there? What's wrong?"

They said, "A crippled girl just got healed!"

I said, "Well, tell her to come up here and give a testimony for Jesus. He's the One Who did it."

A little girl about 14 years old stepped out and started walking down the aisle. She was shaking and crying. She looked perfectly normal to me. There was a boy, about 17 years old, walking with her who was beside himself, too. He was yelling, "This is my crippled sister. I helped her come in here. I take her everywhere and help her get out of the car. She's crippled!"

When they got to the front, the girl walked up on the platform. She was trembling, and her little body was hot.

I put my arm around her and said, "Well, little darling, just tell the people what happened to you."

She said, "I don't know. I was just sitting there and, all of a sudden, my crippled legs began to turn warm. They turned from warm to hot. And when they turned hot, I felt some kind of power going into my legs. I reached down and pushed myself up. When I did, both legs went completely normal. They straightened out totally!"

She was walking just as normally as anybody else. God made both legs completely normal! That's a miracle.

Doing miracles is *not* God's number one way to heal people. God's number one way to heal you is for you to believe Him yourself. You have to believe that the Lord Jesus Christ is your healer. It's you, the Bible, Jesus, and the Holy Ghost.

Make up your mind right now that Jesus is your *personal* healer. You were born into the family of God when you accepted Jesus as your personal Savior. He has been the Savior of the world for two thousand years, but it did not benefit you until you made Him your *personal* Savior. Jesus is the healer. But knowing that will not help you until you accept Him as your *personal* healer.

You do it by faith, the same way you received forgiveness from your sins when you first trusted Jesus. How did you know you were forgiven? Did the guilt leave? Did you have a deep sense of peace? Did the guilt try to return? It often does. Did you claim 1 John 1:9, that if you confess your sins, He is faithful and just to forgive you your sins, and to cleanse you from all unrighteousness? If you claimed that, and continued to claim that, you were eventually established in the truth of your salvation. At that point no demon from hell could talk you out of your faith in Jesus as your Savior.

The same process applies to developing your faith in Jesus as your *personal* healer. When doubts come, claim 1 Peter 2:24, that by His stripes (or lashings) you were healed.

Put Jesus in the now. Talk like He's healing you right now. Talk that way all the time, for the rest of your life. You can live without sickness and disease. God doesn't want you to be sick.

The healing power of the Lord Jesus Christ is a gift of the Church. It is a *free* gift to the Church. It is a gift that is given to *you* to take care of any kind of affliction or infirmity that you have.

7

The Winds of God Bring Revival

The Spirit of God ministers through His nine gifts. He melts hardened hearts and causes sinners to repent. He always knows exactly what to do to get the job done, whether He's planning a revival for one person, a whole city, or an entire nation.

"Jesus Is Real Anyway"

I was having dinner one night with a big shot, New York type of guy. This man was an atheist. We had just walked out of a business meeting and sat down in a restaurant to have dinner. When I picked up the menu I said, "Well, praise the Lord."

He said, "Mr. Hayes, I don't believe in that kind of stuff."

I glanced up and thought, "Good Lord. This is going to be a long night." I was going to have to eat dinner with him and couldn't even talk about Jesus. I said, "To each his own."

Later I asked him, "Can I ask you a question? You've been telling me all these things and talking and talking. Let me talk a minute. Why don't you believe in God?"

"Well," he said, "people say God is a God of love. That's what I've heard all of my life: God is a God of love. My son is 14 years old and a dope addict. My wife is an alcoholic. That's what I'm going home to tonight:

a dope addict and an alcoholic. I'm telling you, Mr. Hayes, if God is a God of love, He forgot to stop at my house. I live in hell with a 14-year-old, dope-addict son and an alcoholic wife."

I gave him my testimony about how God had saved me. It ran off him like water off a duck's back.

He said, "Well, it may be good for you, but it's not good for me." So we paid our check and left the restaurant.

As we were walking up the sidewalk heading toward the meeting room again, all of a sudden, I grabbed him by the arm, twisted him around, pointed my finger in his face and said, "Mister, it doesn't make any difference what you believe. Jesus is real anyway. The Lord told me to tell you if you don't introduce Him to your wife and son, the whole bunch of you are going to go to hell, and He's going to hold you responsible for it. *You.*" And I turned around and walked off. The Holy Ghost has nerve. Man, He is bold.

Now this guy was a well-known lecturer. He's not like me — every word is in place. But after I turned around and walked off, he stood there dumbfounded. He looked like somebody had hit him in the head with a stick. I walked on over to the meeting room. He came in and sat down at his desk. Again, the Holy Ghost started rising up in me. I began to weep. And this wasn't a gospel meeting, it was a business meeting. But the tears began to stream down my face and the love of God (faith worketh by love) began to saturate me. The Lord said, "Walk over there and lay your hands on him and pray for his life right now."

Weeping, I stumbled across the floor of the meeting room to his desk and said, "Mister, Jesus wants me to pray for your life. Bow your head and close your eyes."

I put my hands on top of his head and said, "Jesus touch this man."

He said, "Ah, — oh. . . ." At that moment, he broke and began to weep. I took him through the sinner's prayer and the Lord saved him.

He said, "Oh, God, I feel so good. What's in your hands? When you laid your hands on me, power shot through me. It felt like electricity. It just broke me."

I said, "That's the Holy Ghost coming into you."

He went home that night and told his alcoholic wife, "Honey, the Lord wants to save you."

She said, "Are you drunk, too?"

"No, I got saved. Jesus saved me. I met this strange man who has some kind of power flowing through his hands. When he put his hands on me, the power shot through me. I broke and wept. I gave my life to Jesus. Can you believe that?"

She said, "No, I can't believe it. But if God can save you, an atheist for years, He can save anybody. I think I'll get saved myself."

His wife got saved. His son got saved and delivered from dope and is an evangelist now. About 30 members of their family have been saved, too.

You say, "Well, Brother Norvel, you have a good ministry."

I gave the man my testimony. I told him everything I knew about God, and it didn't even phase him. But all of a sudden, when the gift of faith came, it made all the difference in the world. It's the ministry of the Holy Spirit, not Norvel Hayes' ministry. I was only a vessel. The Holy Spirit knows how to melt an atheist's heart like butter.

Confronting Killers

I used to minister in penitentiaries a lot. At Colorado State Penitentiary, the inmates had been killing people. Several people had been killed with knives, and the officials couldn't catch the murderer. So they called me and asked if I would come and speak to these men. I agreed to come.

Before I went into the prison they took everything out of my pockets and warned me, "You may die in there. Those men have already killed several people." I said, "Well, I'm going in anyway."

The inmates began to laugh at me as soon as I walked in. So I just started talking to them about Jesus. I walked across in front of them and talked to them about the Lord. The longer I talked the more they laughed.

All of a sudden, the power came. I said, "What are you laughing at me for, you dummies? You're the ones who are in here, not me!" If it had not been for the Holy Ghost, I never would have said that.

I went on, "You over there. Why did you rape that girl? Now you've got 65 years. And you, sitting here, why did you kill that man? Now you've got 200 years. And you over there, you bank robber. Why don't you work in a job, you old lazy thing?" All the laughing stopped the moment the power came.

That power, the gift of faith, caused me to have supernatural faith in God and say words that I wouldn't dare say without the Holy Ghost. I'm pretty bold myself, but I'm not that bold. But when the Holy Spirit comes on you, you don't see anything except victory. I forgot about some of them being killers and other types of criminals. It didn't even enter my mind. I could see nothing but victory.

When you look out of the eyes of the Holy Ghost on the inside of you, you can see nothing except victory. There's nothing but victory in the knowledge of the Holy Ghost. He lives in you, waiting and hoping that you'll trust Him. If you'll trust Him according to the Word, He'll manifest Himself.

The gift of faith gives you an abundance of power in your life to do something that God wants done. You couldn't do it before — sometimes you don't even have the knowledge of *how* to do it. But when God comes on you and gives you the faith, you do it.

The prison officials had already told me, "You can't give an invitation, Mr. Hayes. You can't touch anybody. And you can't call people down front."

I asked, "Well, can I say anything I want to then?"

They told me that was OK.

So I had the prisoners bow their heads. I told the whole prison, "God is looking for men with backbone. God does not want any weaklings. Any of you guys got any backbone about you? If so, bow your head and close your eyes right now." And they did! (It's a good thing I had the Holy Ghost with me!) I said, "Any of you who want to accept Jesus and get a brand new life, hold up your hand."

As God is my witness, when I said that, one of the prisoners, a big guy who had been laughing and pointing his finger, was the first one God hit. A glory cloud came in over that prison. Those prisoners began to weep everywhere. They wept and held up their hands all over the room to get saved.

After the meeting, a prison official said, "We have a banquet set up for you. You can talk to the prisoners for one hour in another building." So I went over there, and for one hour I talked to the prisoners.

I was warned to meet with only two prisoners at a time because the murders had occurred when four or five people were in a group. All of a sudden, four of them would walk away, and one of them would be left with a knife in him, lying in a pool of blood. And the murderer had never been discovered.

But the whole hour I was alone with all those prisoners, they came up to me, shook hands with me, and said, "We want you to come back. You tell us the truth." "I sure appreciate those words you said." "Oh, God, what you said helped me. I could see myself."

You say, "Well, that's a pretty good prison ministry, Brother Norvel."

Yes. That's the ministry of the Holy Ghost. Those men laughed at me for 20 minutes. But when the power came on me, they stopped laughing. They were like little lambs listening to every word.

Are You Available?

These examples show the way the gift of faith works to start revival. Are you available for this gift? Would you like to have it? Would you? You have to tell God you want it.

Are you available to stop in the middle of the sidewalk and say, "Yes, Lord!" and deliver God's message? Are you available to walk over to a woman, a real nice lady, the wife of the man that invited you to speak, and scream at her, "What are you doing sitting here?" Are you available to deliver God's Message under the gift of faith, that abundance of power that gets the job done and knocks people out of darkness by making them think straight?

If you're not available, God will never give you the gift of faith. You have to be available *now*. You have to be available to deliver God's message — *what* He wants done, *when* He wants it done, and *how* He wants it done. He'll try you a few times, but if you don't yield to Him and do it, He won't bother you anymore. It doesn't mean you're not a Christian; you're just not available.

If you're available for the gift of faith, say, "Jesus, I make myself available for the gift of faith. I will obey You if You want to use me like that. I will obey You in the gift of faith."

Hold up your right hand and say, "Lord, send the power to me. Cause me to do something that's in Your will that I couldn't do before. Thank You, Lord, for the gift of faith. In Jesus' name, I receive it with thanksgiving. I accept it. And I accept being used by You as the Spirit wills, not as I will. In Jesus' name. Amen."

The Course of a Nation Can Be Turned

You may go for months and nothing happens. Then, all of a sudden, it happens. When God can manifest the gift of faith through someone, it could cause salvation to come to one person or to thousands of people. One manifestation of the gift of faith, or any one of the gifts of the Spirit, can cause the course of a nation to be turned. Think about it: one gift of the Spirit can change history.

PART IV
The Revived Church

As the hart panteth after the water brooks, so panteth my soul after thee, O God. My soul thirsteth for God, for the living God: when shall I come and appear before God?

Psalm 42:1,2

8

Hungry to Receive From God

Bill Kaiser, Director of the Bible School at Word of Faith in Dallas, Texas, explained how a heart hungry for God sparked the Azusa Street revival.

"Toward the close of the 1900s, God found a group of hungry-hearted Bible college students in Topeka, Kansas. Charles Parham was the director. He had to leave for three days to preach a New Year's meeting in Kansas City and told his students to research the Word of God concerning the Holy Spirit while he was gone.

"Brother Parham returned on New Year's Day of 1901. His students came together and told him what they had found. They saw that every time the Holy Spirit was poured out, the initial evidence was the gift of tongues.

"One young student seemed to be more hungry than the rest. Her name was Agnes Osman. She quickly stepped forward and said, 'Lay hands on me that I might receive the Holy Spirit and the gift of tongues.'

"Brother Parham was reluctant to do so, because he had never prayed for anyone to have this experience before. She pressed him. She insisted. She had enough hunger to press in.

"Finally, Brother Parham laid hands on her. God honored that prayer of faith. She began to speak in a language that she had never studied, experienced, or heard before. She received the gift of tongues.

"For two days nothing happened. On the third day, twelve more students received the gift of tongues. Word soon spread. Reporters came.

"One rabbi came to the school and listened to Sister Osman. He said, 'That's a miracle. That's the most precious expression of the Twenty-third Psalm I have ever heard in my native Hebrew.' This young lady had never studied Hebrew.

"The Bible college lost the lease on their building. Charles Parham ministered around Kansas for a time. Later, he went to Houston, Texas, where he started another Bible college in 1905. There he met William Seymour, a precious Holiness preacher. Brother Seymour received the gift of tongues. He was destined to preach the Azusa Street revival.

"A visiting lady pastor invited Brother Seymour to be her associate pastor in California. He went and preached his first sermon on the miracle of Pentecost and the gift of tongues. The congregation rejected him, and he couldn't stay. But he didn't let that stop him. He began to share in his own home. More and more people came. Finally, he had to stand on the front porch and preach to the people out on the lawn, because the house wasn't big enough. People began to receive the gift of tongues.

"They had to find more space, so they searched and found a place at 312 Azusa Street. It was a half burned-out building that had first been a Methodist church, then a lumber yard. After the lumber yard burned down, the building was abandoned. That's the humble place where they started meeting.

"They didn't have pews — they sat on nail kegs. They didn't have a pulpit. But this precious William Seymour would kneel and pray — and the glory would fall. People got healed and delivered. For three years, three times a day, seven days a week, they had revival at Azusa Street. It all started with a hungry heart. Hallelujah — Azusa Street lives on today!"

Revival is hunger for God. You've got to get hungry. Get so hungry for revival to hit your church that you pray and cry out to God until He sends it. Don't give up. He'll send it.

If you're a pastor, go to the sanctuary by yourself in the afternoon. Study your Bible, walk the floor, and pray. Ask God's best for your congregation. Show God you're a first-class pastor and shepherd. Tell Him you want His first-class manifestations for your congregation. Say, "I want God's best for my people, Jesus. Jesus, I want every sick person in this congregation to be healed by Your mighty, divine healing power. Your healing power is welcome in this church, Lord. Let Your mighty power and glory come in here and bless this flock. Let Your miracle-working power come in here, Lord."

Ask God for the great benefits that He has promised you and the Church. Tell Him the benefits you are not receiving and claim them in Jesus' name by faith. Walk the floor and speak them into existence. Believe God, and He will do it for you. He'll give you gifts from heaven. It is not God's will to withhold any good thing from any of His children or any of His churches. God loves the Church so much. Jesus is the Great Shepherd. He really loves the Church. He wants all these beautiful things happening in the Church all the time.

Let the Holy Spirit Have His Way

As soon as we figure out Who we're serving and realize who we are in Him, we can have revival all the time.

When God wants to have revival, let Him have it. God has started a lot of revivals in churches, and they just closed it down. The next time you feel the Holy Spirit start a revival spirit burning down in your bones, don't close it down. Keep on going, preach like a house on fire. Let the Spirit of God work.

Be willing to obey the Spirit. When God speaks to you, be willing to go ahead and flow with it. It's fine to have some kind of basic outline of what you might do in your service, but with the Holy Ghost, you will often wind up not following even a basic plan.

Put the Holy Ghost in charge. If you are a pastor, don't worry about your service and how you're going to run it. If the Holy Ghost is in charge, you'll know the moves to make and when to make them. You'll know, that you know, that you know. Let the Spirit of God be God. If He wants to heal people during a song, let Him work.

The main thing to do is to find out what the Spirit of God wants done. The Holy Spirit is heaven's representative on the earth. Decisions made by God and Jesus are always worked out on the earth by the Holy Spirit. After He gets the information from heaven of what They'd like to have done, He has another job — getting the plan over to you. His success depends upon the condition of your human spirit.

If you haven't been praying, and you don't recognize what the Holy Spirit is trying to do, you will never pick it up. And the Holy Spirit will never, never shove anything from heaven down your throat. You have to pick it up, then believe it. The price for everything from heaven has already been paid. It's all free, but it's all precious and all to be respected — everything. If you don't have a high regard and a high respect for the gifts of the Spirit, you'll never get them. God will see to it that you'll never get them.

Be sensitive to the Spirit. Some of the greatest healing services I've ever had were ones when nobody sang a song, nobody did anything. We were just quiet. But my hands were heavily anointed. The Lord would say to me, "Tonight, I want to operate. I want to perform surgery tonight. Don't let other people say a word."

At other times, you might sing songs and play instruments just like in an old-time Pentecostal healing meeting. It's the same thing in any of Jesus' churches: you have to learn how to be led by the Spirit of God. Worship and prayer get you close to God; the closer you are to Him the better you can be led.

In 1965 Jesus walked into Brother Kenneth Hagin's room, sat down in a chair, and talked to him for an hour and a half. He talked about the gifts of the Spirit and about the Church. Jesus said, "Most of what you call full gospel churches don't have anything left except tongues and interpretation of tongues. They're growing cold." And Jesus let Brother Hagin know, "I don't like it . . . . I'm going to raise up people who will glorify the Church, glorify God, and glorify heaven."

Jesus says, **If the Son therefore shall make you free, ye shall be free indeed** (John 8:36). We need to be free from denominational, planned services. Just let the Spirit of God do what He wants to do and bless people all over the world like He wants to.

Revival Brings Power to the Church

The winds of revival hit with full force during the Dallas seminar, creating a giant wave of healings, miracles, and salvations. Because of satellite TV, millions of people of all denominations were caught up in the revival spirit. Churches around the world reported marked increases in attendance. The revival fire hit and was spreading fast.

There are three main things to look for in a revival. First, the Church is lifted up, cleansed from sin, and restored. It takes its rightful place of importance. Second, sinners are drawn in and are saved by the power of the Holy Spirit. And third, Jesus, once again, becomes the main love in the life of every believer.

Revival will bless the Church and restore it back to its rightful position. For many decades it's been only a place where you go on Sunday. The Church has lost some of its power. Revival puts power back in the Church.

A church building should be a house of prayer, a house of victory, a house of love, and a house of restoration.

Many times you see a beautiful building sitting on the corner calling itself a church. You hear people say, "I go to church there; I'm Methodist." Or, "I go to church here; I'm Baptist," and so forth. "I go there every Sunday morning."

The Church is not in its rightful place like that. I want to see the Church revived and restored back in its rightful place. Then Jesus will have a chance to be Himself and set people free. The Bible says, **If the Son therefore shall make you free, ye shall be free indeed** (John 8:36).

God says, **. . . mine house shall be called an house of prayer** (Is. 56:7). People can go to a powerful, Jesus-filled church, pray and make contact with God.

God's house must be a house of prayer. The heart-felt fervent prayer of a righteous man makes contact with God. (James 5:16.) This place of prayer is where victory is found. It's where peace, salvation, healings, and miracles are found. When you make contact with God, bad nerves disappear. People find peace for their minds — peace that passes all understanding — when they make contact with God. (Phil. 4:7.) Revival and the spirit of prayer go hand in hand. The spirit of prayer comes out of your belly with a burning power. It changes things.

When peace comes and continues inside of you, then you know you've prayed through. Pray until you know that you know. Pray until you get victory!

The revived church is a house of victory. It's where you go to hear the Word of God in teaching, preaching, and song. God wants to make people strong by building a foundation based on the knowledge of Christ in them. People must know who they are in Christ.

In a church full of power there should be strong fellowship to teach you to live with and to love one another. A New Testament church should be filled with love, filled with the presence of God. If the right kind of atmosphere exists, people will want to go there.

And God's house should be like a hospital. All the fruits of the Spirit and the gifts of the Spirit should be in operation, restoring those who are lost and healing those who are hurt.

Security in Jesus

The most important thing to come out of revival is for people to find security in Jesus and in His Church. Then people's lives become productive and strong. The works of the devil are unraveled in a praying, revived church. The devil can't stand a praying church. He knows his work is stopped.

A true revival in God causes the whole Church to respond to righteousness, not just an arm of the Church. This revival is international in scale. Baptists, Methodists, and Pentecostals are being touched by God. He's in the healing, saving, and delivering business for everyone.

For example, a black woman was called out of the audience during the Word of Faith satellite conference. She was a Baptist woman who loved Jesus. I came down to her, laid my hands on her, and said, "You foul spirit of blindness, in Jesus' name, come out of her!" At that moment she fell back on the floor and lay there weeping. When she got up, her eyes were normal. She walked on stage and said, "I can see, I can see!" These are the kinds of things that happen during revival.

The New Waves Bring What Is Lacking

There is some truth about certain kinds of ministries and certain kinds of blessings coming in waves. And if you'll notice, they usually last about one decade.

In the late 1940s the healing ministries started. A wave of healing glory came over America. God had several healing evangelists; the healing wave was strong. That lasted about 10 to 12 years.

Then there was a time when a great emphasis was put on the baptism of the Holy Spirit. The Full Gospel Business Men's Fellowship meetings were a powerful tool used by God to get denominational people baptized in the Holy Spirit. Of course, that's still going on. But there was a great wave of it for about 15 years.

I was an international director of Full Gospel Business Men's Fellowship for several years. And I remember when 30 or 40 directors would be in the altar room praying and working with people, getting them baptized in the Holy Spirit. This would go on every night until midnight during the entire convention.

Next the Word people came along with a great wave of teaching. When I was growing up, nobody had much respect for the Bible teacher. That was a great shame, because it's one of the offices of the Church. (1 Cor. 12:28.)

Remember this: You learn from the teacher. That's the reason God set the office of teacher as one of the five offices of the Church. That's one of the reasons this revival kicked off the way it did. I'm a teacher, and I was teaching on the gifts of the Spirit.

The teaching ministry has lasted 10 to 20 years and is still flourishing. Some people say the faith movement is beginning to wane. God would never stop working through faith because God is a faith God. Hebrews 11:6 says, . . . **without faith it is impossible to please him** (God). God doesn't work if faith is not shown. He'll never get tired of faith.

All of these waves are still going on. When God sends a wave of revival across this country or around the world, I don't think it ever dies. But it does seem that He'll do something for 10 or 12 years, then He'll start doing something else really strong.

If you'll notice, the new waves supply what is being left out of the Church. God is so merciful. He doesn't want any lack in the Church. For example, the late 1950s and early 1960s started a great surge of tongues because it had been left out. A few Pentecostals had it, but basically the Church body had been without it.

This newest wave is bringing back the miracles and healings of the New Testament Church. I believe this revival is ushering in great financial blessings to the Church on a scale we've never seen before. It is thrusting us into New Testament miracles. Prepare your heart, yield to the spirit of prayer, and see God's power come into your life in a revived fashion. God's power is available every day to everyone. You don't have to be a preacher or revivalist to get God to move for you. All you need is a repentant heart and a hunger for God.

How To Get Revival

Revival comes as a result of prayer and repentance. Pray until God comes, then weep over your sins. Tell God all about them. Ask Him to cleanse you and restore you. Pray that God will cleanse your heart and rid you of worldliness. You'll know you're home when you feel the convicting power of the Holy Ghost begin to work. Once the Church is cleansed, then the sinners can be brought in.

When you are seeking God, remember to ask for a revival for your city as well as for your church. Without one, your city will go to hell. Unless you have a vision of people going to hell, you won't do anything to rescue them. Start praying individually and corporately for a city-wide revival in all the churches. When the Holy Spirit comes, and He will come, let the revival blow like the wind.

Revival begins with hunger. The hunger brings the power.

Lord, let every person who reads this book hunger for revival — hunger for God to visit their church, visit their home, heal their little children as they sleep in their beds. Let people be hungry for God every day, not just on Sunday. Let them get hungry for heaven. Let them get hungry for pure love that's real, hungry for Jesus. In Jesus' name. Amen.

Why Have Revival?

Revival makes a church red hot and aflame with the Spirit. Some people believe the way they want to believe, instead of believing what Matthew, Mark, Luke, and John say. Then when death comes knocking on their door, they'd like to flow really quick to where the blessing is. It's not that easy.

If you want Jesus to be the Jesus of the New Testament, you can't go to a cold church and get it. You have to go somewhere where the uncompromised Word of God is being preached, taught, and expounded upon.

If you aren't going to a church that expounds upon Jesus as your healer, you probably won't get healed. Jesus has to hear something. Faith has a voice.

In the Church of the Lord Jesus Christ, the New Testament Church, an altar is a sacred thing. An altar is a place of prayer, repentance, and worship. Weeping all that junk out of you around the altar brings God on the scene. An altar is holy, clean, sacred, and true. You can see in the Old and New Testaments that God, Jesus, and the Holy Spirit all love the altar. They love an altar in a church where people can come before God in Jesus' name. The altar represents Him. When you come to meet Him, He meets you, because Jesus is the Head of the Church, and He loves His Church.

An altar is in your heart, too. You can stop and pray anywhere, anytime. Close your eyes, shut out the world, and enter into the presence of the Living God. If you don't know Jesus, pray the prayer below and pray it loudly. Speak it boldly, but humbly.

Oh, Lord God, I come to Your throne in Jesus' name. As a sinner, someone lost and without hope in this world, I ask Jesus to come and be my Lord. (Rom. 10:9,10.) Break up the foundations of sin in my life. Cleanse me and seal me for eternity with Your sweet Spirit. Baptize me in Your Holy Spirit. (Acts 2.)

Oh, God, forgive my sins. They are as scarlet. But You can make them white as snow. (Is. 1:18.) I lay my sins on the altar now. Send down Your fire and consume them, oh, God. (Heb. 12:29.)

Teach me, like a little child, to lift my eyes toward heaven and call You my Father. Be my healer, keep me revived and